Total Person Toolbox

Words that Work

■ ■ ■

By Prince Handley

University of Excellence Press

Copyright © 2014 by Prince Handley
All Rights Reserved.

UNIVERSITY OF EXCELLENCE PRESS
Los Angeles ■ London ■ Tel Aviv

ISBN-13: 978-0692377055
ISBN-10: 0692377050

Printed in the U.S.A.

First Edition

The only Toolbox book you need!

TABLE OF CONTENTS

FOREWORD

Affirmations are powerful ... IF you are affirming the truth in line with God's promised blessings. The definition of affirmation is as follows: *"Something declared to be true; a positive statement or judgment."* It is a means of influencing—of reinforcing—our own behavior or beliefs.

An affirmation is simply a **declaration** of our fixed intent—**based upon what we hold to be true**—to succeed, progress, achieve, develop or mature in a preselected area of our life, profession or relationships.

If you know that what you are declaring is true—without a doubt—you have only to **continue in faith with patience**. You can actually **begin thanking God** for the answer. Giving thanks to God is very important as it shows God you believe Him, and that you believe His promises to you are true and established in Eternity.

*"Be anxious about nothing, but in everything by prayer and earnest request **with thanksgiving**, let your requests be made known to God. And the peace of God, which is so far above all human understanding, will guard your hearts and minds through Messiah Jesus."*

In other words, you can KNOW you have what you're declaring because you are saying and believing God's promises—promises that He made to you—saying them back to Him, and **thanking Him for the answer**.

You will have **peace while you wait in patience with faith** for what you have declared.

What is it you want or need from God? I have selected four major areas of life from which you can choose key affirmations based upon God's promises to you. These four major areas are as follows:

- How to be whole

- How to be healed

- How to receive God's power

- How to prosper

When you operate successfully in all of these areas you can accomplish anything else in life.

The affirmations in this book have been distributed for 35 years in many nations—in many languages—and among many groups of people. This book is also an excellent gift for people who are without a working knowledge of scripture ... and who have no knowledge of how to access God's MIRACLE working power.

For example, scores of people received the Baptism in the Holy Spirit and spoke in tongues from ONE—the same—piece of paper that had the affirmations on the section in this book titled, *How to Receive God's Power*.

This book is dedicated to Yashar.

A rose with no thorns.

Total Person Toolbox

Words that Work

■ ■ ■

AFFIRMATIONS OF GREATNESS

Affirmations are powerful ... IF you are affirming the truth in line with God's **promised** blessings. The definition of affirmation is as follows: *"Something declared to be true; a positive statement or judgment."* It is a means of influencing—of reinforcing—our own behavior or beliefs.

An affirmation is simply a **declaration** of our fixed intent—**based upon what we hold to be true**—to succeed, progress, achieve, develop or mature in a preselected area of our life, profession or relationships.

If you know that what you are declaring is true—without a doubt—you have only to **continue in faith with patience**. You can actually **begin thanking God** for the answer. Giving thanks to God is very important as it shows God you believe Him, and that you believe His promises to you are true and established in Eternity.

*"Be anxious about nothing, but in everything by prayer and earnest request **with thanksgiving**, let your requests be made known to God. And the peace of God, which is so far above all human understanding, will guard your hearts and minds through Messiah Jesus."*

In other words, you can KNOW you have what you're declaring because you are saying and believing God's promises—promises that He made to you—saying them back to Him, and thanking Him for the answer. You will have **peace while you wait in patience with faith** for what you have declared.

What is it you want or need from God? I have selected four major areas of life from which you can choose key affirmations based upon God's promises to you. These four major areas are as follows:

8

- How to be whole

- How to be healed

- How to receive God's power

- How to prosper

When you operate successfully in all of these areas you can accomplish anything else in life.

Here we go ... listen up!

How to be Whole

GOD CREATED THE UNIVERSE
BECAUSE HE HAD A PLAN
"In the beginning God created the heaven and the earth."
[Genesis 1:1]

GOD CREATED THE FIRST MAN NAMED ADAM
"So God created man in his own image."
[Genesis 1:27]

GOD MADE THE UNIVERSE FOR THE
EARTH AND THE EARTH FOR MAN
"Multiply, and replenish the earth, and subdue it."
[Genesis 1:28]

MAN WAS NOT TO EAT OF THE
TREE OF KNOWLEDGE OF GOOD AND EVIL
"In the day you eat thereof, you shall surely die."
[Genesis 2:17]

THE DEVIL LIED TO ADAM
CAUSING HIM TO DISOBEY GOD
"And the serpent said ... 'You shall not surely die'."
[Genesis 3:4]

**ADAM—THE FIRST MAN—DISOBEYED GOD
BRINGING DEATH AND SIN TO ALL MEN**

"By one man sin entered into the world, and death by sin."
[Romans 5:12]

**JESUS CHRIST WAS THE "GOD-MAN"
HE OBEYED GOD ... BRINGING LIFE**

"By the obedience of one shall many be made righteous."
[Romans 5:19]

**CHRIST IS GOD'S SON
HE CAME TO EARTH IN HUMAN FLESH**

"This is my beloved Son ... hear him."
[Matthew 3:17 / 17:5]

**HE WAS BEATEN AND NAILED
TO A WOODEN CROSS FOR YOU**

"So Christ was once offered to bear the sins of many."
[Hebrews 9:28]

**GOD SENT HIS SON TO EARTH
AS *PAYMENT* FOR YOUR SINS**

"While we were yet sinners, Christ died for us."
[Romans 5:8]

**GOD PROVED HIS LOVE
HE GAVE HIS ONLY SON FOR YOU**

"For God so loved the world ... he gave his only Son."
[John 3:16]

GOD'S GIFT TO YOU IS FREE
YOU CANNOT EARN IT OR BUY IT

"The gift of God is eternal life thru Jesus Christ our Lord."
[Romans 6:23]

GOD RAISED HIS SON FROM THE DEAD
HE IS ALIVE TO SAVE YOU

"Christ died for our sins ... was buried ... rose again."
[2 Corinthians 15:3-4]

YOU CAN BE SAVED BY TURNING FROM SIN
AND BELIEVING ON CHRIST

"Repent, and believe the Good News."
[Mark 1:15]

REPENT

"Repent ... turn to God, so that your sins may be wiped out."
[Acts 3:19]

BELIEVE

"He that believes on the Son has everlasting life."
[John 3:36]

ASK CHRIST TO SAVE YOU NOW
ASK HIM INTO YOUR LIFE

"Whoever calls upon the name of the Lord will be saved."
[Romans 10:13]

AFTER YOU ARE SAVED

WHAT SHOULD YOU DO AFTER YOU ARE SAVED?
"Be baptized ... and receive the gift of the Holy Spirit."
[Acts 2:38]

WHY SHOULD YOU BE BAPTIZED IN WATER?
" ... the answer of a clean conscience toward God."
[I Peter 3:21]

**WHY SHOULD YOU RECEIVE THE GIFT
OF THE HOLY SPIRIT?**
"You shall receive power after the Holy Spirit is upon
you."
[Acts 1:8]

**WHAT WILL HAPPEN WHEN YOU RECEIVE
THE GIFT OF THE HOLY SPIRIT?**
" ... they spoke with other tongues."
[Acts 2:4 / 10:46 / 19:6]

**WHAT WILL CHRIST'S BLOOD THAT WAS
SHED ON THE CROSS DO FOR YOU?**
"Cleanse from dead works to serve the living God."
[Hebrews 9:14]

GOD PROMISED TO SAVE YOUR
HOUSEHOLD IF YOU BELIEVE
"You shall be saved, and your house."
[Acts 16:31]

ALL HAVE SINNED
ALL PEOPLE NEED TO BE SAVED
"For all have sinned, and come short of the glory of
God."
[Romans 3:23]

TELL PEOPLE ABOUT JESUS
WHAT HE CAN DO FOR THEM
"Go into all the world, and preach the Good News."
[Mark 16:15]

THERE IS NO OTHER NAME
BY WHICH PEOPLE CAN BE SAVED
"Neither is there salvation in any other."
[Acts 4:12 / John 14:6]

READ GOD'S WORD AND PRAY EVERY DAY:
MORNING & NIGHT
"You will make your way prosperous with good
success."
[Joshua 1:8]

IF YOU CONFESS YOUR SINS TO GOD
HE WILL FORGIVE YOU
"He is faithful ... to forgive us our sins, and to cleanse
us."
[1 John 1:9]

YOU ARE A NEW PERSON WHEN YOU ARE SAVED

"Old things are passed away: all things become new."
[2 Corinthians 5:17]

IF YOU KNOW JESUS, YOU DO NOT HAVE TO BE SICK

"He took our illnesses and carried away our diseases."
[Matthew 8:17]

IF YOU KNOW JESUS, YOU DO NOT HAVE TO BE POOR

"He became poor, that you ... might become rich."
[2 Corinthians 8:9]

IF YOU KNOW JESUS, YOU DO NOT HAVE TO BE OPPRESSED

"God anointed Jesus ... who went about healing all that were oppressed of the devil."
[Acts 10:38]

IF YOU KNOW JESUS, YOU CAN BE A LEADER IN THE WORLD

"The Lord shall make you the head, and not the tail."
[Deuteronomy 28:13]

How to be Healed

GOD CREATED THE FIRST MAN NAMED ADAM
"So God created man in his own image."
[Genesis 1:27]

THE DEVIL LIED TO ADAM
CAUSING HIM TO DISOBEY GOD
"And the serpent said ...'You shall not surely die'."
[Genesis 3:4]

ADAM DISOBEYED GOD
BRINGING SIN AND DEATH TO ALL MEN
"By one man sin entered into the world, and death by sin."
[Romans 5:12]

PHYSICAL DEATH AND SICKNESS
ARE THE RESULT OF SIN
"Death passed upon all men, for all have sinned."
[Romans 5:12]

SIN SEPARATED MAN
FROM GOD'S HEALTH AND LIFE
"For all have sinned and come short of the glory of God."
[Romans 3:23]

GOD'S SON, JESUS THE MESSIAH
CAME TO EARTH TO HEAL THE SEPARATION
"He came to destroy the works of the devil."
[1 John 3:8]

GOD'S SON WAS BEATEN AND
NAILED TO A CROSS STAKE FOR YOU
"For God so loved the world, that he gave his only ...
Son."
[John 3:16]

GOD SENT HIS SON TO EARTH
AS PAYMENT FOR YOUR SINS
"The LORD has laid on him the sin of us all."
[Isaiah 53:6]

ON THE CROSS STAKE YESHUA (JESUS)
TOOK YOUR SICKNESS, DISEASE, AND PAIN
"He has borne our sicknesses and diseases, and
carried our pains."
[Isaiah 53:4]

HIS BODY WAS PUNISHED AND HIS BLOOD
PAID THE PRICE: FOR HEALING
"With his stripes (bruises) we are healed."
[Isaiah 53:5]

GOD RAISED HIS SON FROM THE DEAD
HE IS ALIVE TO HEAL YOU
" Messiah died for our sins ... was buried ... rose
again."
[2 Corinthians 15:3-4]

JESUS NEVER REFUSED HEALING TO ANYONE
"Yeshua went about ... healing all that were oppressed
of the devil."
[Acts 10:38]

MESSIAH JESUS' HEALING NATURE
NEVER CHANGES
"Yeshua, the Messiah, the same yesterday, and today, and forever."
[Hebrews 13:8]

GOD PROMISES HEALING AND
FORGIVENESS OF SINS TO YOU
"Who forgives all your sins: who heals all your diseases."
[Psalm 103:3]

GOD WANTS TO HEAL YOU AND TO SAVE YOU
FROM DISEASE AND SIN
"I am the LORD that heals you."
[Exodus 15:26]

GOD WILL HEAL YOU AND KEEP
YOU HEALTHY IF YOU SERVE HIM
"You shall serve the LORD ... and I will take sickness away."
[Exodus 23:25]

ASK THE LORD JESUS TO HEAL YOU NOW
ASK HIM TO SAVE YOU
"Call upon me in the day of trouble: I will deliver you."
[Psalm 50:15]

FACTS ABOUT HEALING

**THE DEVIL WANTS TO HURT YOU \
AND MAKE YOU SICK**
"The thief comes ... to steal, and to kill, and to destroy."
[John 10:10]

**JESUS WANTS TO HELP YOU
AND MAKE YOU WHOLE**
"I am come that they might have life ... abundantly."
[John 10:10]

JESUS WILL GIVE YOU POWER OVER THE DEVIL
"I give you power ... over all the power of the enemy."
[Luke 10:19]

**CONTINUE TO TRUST ONLY CHRIST
AS YOUR LORD — TURN FROM SIN**
"Stop sinning, so that nothing worse may happen to
you."
[John 5:14]

DO NOT RECEIVE SICKNESS OR PAIN
"Resist the devil, and he will flee from you."
[James 4:7]

**RESIST SATAN AND HIS WORKS
BY SPEAKING GOD'S WORD**
"Jesus said unto him (the devil), 'It is written ....'"
[Matthew 4:1-11]

**SOME PEOPLE ARE BOUND
BY A DEMON SPIRIT OF INFIRMITY**
"Cast out the spirits with a word."
[Luke 13:11-13 / Mark 9:25 / Matthew 8:16]

**DEMONS AND SICKNESS MUST
SUBMIT TO THE NAME OF JESUS**
"Lord, even the demons submit to us in your name."
[Luke 10:17]

**THE NAME "JESUS" IS ABOVE THE NAMES
OF "SICKNESS" OR "PAIN"**
"God exalted him and gave him a name above every
name."
[Philippians 2:9]

**COMMAND SICKNESS OR PAIN
TO 'GO AWAY' IN JESUS' NAME**
"Whoever shall say and not doubt shall have what he
says."
[Mark 11:23]

DO NOT ACCEPT SICKNESS OR DISEASE OR PAIN
"He took our infirmities, and carried away our
diseases."
[Matthew 8:17]

**YOU CAN BE HEALED BY SAYING GOD'S WORD
AND BELIEVING IT**
"Confess with your mouth ... and believe in your heart."
[Romans 10:9]

**YOU CAN BE HEALED BY HEARING OR READING
GOD'S WORD**
"He sent his word and healed them."
[Psalm 107:20]

**YOU CAN BE HEALED BY HANDS LAID ON YOU
IN JESUS' NAME**
"(Believers) lay hands on the sick, and they shall
recover."
(Mark 16:18)

**YOU CAN BE HEALED BY
THE ANOINTING WITH OIL**
"Is any(one) sick? ... call for the elders of the church."
[James 5:14-15]

YOU CAN BE HEALED IN BODY, MIND, AND SPIRIT
"Heal me, O Lord, and I shall be healed."
[Jeremiah 17:14]

**YOU CAN BE HEALED BY PROPER
MENTAL ATTITUDE & PRAYER**
"All things are possible to him that believes."
[Mark 9:23]

YOU CAN BE HEALED BY A PRAYER CLOTH PLACED ON YOUR BODY

"The diseases left them, and evil spirits went out of them."

[Acts 19:11-12]

If you want to know more about God and his healing power, study the book, *Health and Healing Complete Guide to Wholeness*, by Prince Handley. (Available at Amazon and other book stores.)

How TO RECEIVE GOD'S POWER

CHRIST WANTS US TO TELL HIS "GOOD NEWS" TO THE WHOLE WORLD

"Go into all the world, and preach the Good News."
[Mark 16:15]

HE PROMISED TO SEND A GIFT OF POWER TO HELP US DO THE WORK

"I send the promise of my Father upon you."
[Luke 24:49 / Acts 1:4]

THE GIFT HE PROMISED US IS THE BAPTISM IN THE HOLY SPIRIT

"John baptized with water: you shall be baptized with God's Spirit."
[Acts 1:5]

THE PROMISE OF THE BAPTISM IN THE HOLY SPIRIT WAS MADE TO YOU

"The promise is unto as many as the Lord our God shall call."
[Acts 2:39]

BAPTISM IN THE SPIRIT IS A GIFT OF POWER

"You shall receive power when the Holy Spirit comes to you."
[Acts 1:8]

MAKE SURE THAT JESUS CHRIST IS YOUR LORD
HE IS THE BAPTIZER
"The same is he which baptizes with the Holy Spirit."
[John 1:33]

JESUS' FOLLOWERS HAD RENEWAL ...
BUT NOT HOLY SPIRIT BAPTISM
"He breathed on them, and said ... 'You receive the
Holy Spirit'."
[John 20:22]

HE TOLD THEM TO WAIT FOR SPIRIT BAPTISM
UNTIL HE WENT TO HEAVEN
"Wait ... until you are clothed with power from on high."
[Luke 24:49]

JESUS WENT BACK TO HEAVEN AND
POURED OUT THE HOLY SPIRIT
"Having received ... the promise, he has poured out ..."
[Acts 2:33]

BECAUSE OF THE BAPTISM YOU CAN DO
GREATER WORKS THAN JESUS
"Greater works shall you do: because I go to my
Father."
[John 14:12]

ALL WHO KNOW JESUS HAVE
THE HOLY SPIRIT OF RENEWAL
"(By) his mercy he saved us ... renewing us by the
Holy Spirit."
[Titus 3:5]

24

ALL WHO KNOW JESUS DO NOT HAVE THE BAPTISM IN THE SPIRIT ... BUT CAN!

"For the promise is unto you ... and unto all that are afar off."
[Acts 2:39]

BAPTISM IN THE SPIRIT CAN HAPPEN AFTER WATER BAPTISM

"Repent, and be baptized ... and you shall receive the gift."
[Acts 2:38]

BAPTISM IN THE SPIRIT CAN HAPPEN BEFORE WATER BAPTISM

"Can any forbid water to these who have received the Holy Spirit?"
[Acts 10:47]

WHAT IS THE FIRST EVIDENCE OF THE BAPTISM IN THE HOLY SPIRIT?

" ... they spoke with tongues."
[Acts 2:1-4 / 10:44-46 / 19:1-6]

SPEAKING IN TONGUES IS NOT SPEAKING A LANGUAGE YOU KNOW

"If I pray in a tongue ... my understanding is unfruitful."
[1 Corinthians 14:14]

SPEAKING IN TONGUES IS THE LANGUAGE OF THE SPIRIT

"If I pray in an unknown tongue, my spirit prays."
[1 Corinthians 14:14]

SPEAKING IN TONGUES HELPS YOU PRAY ACCORDING TO GOD'S WILL
"The spirit intercedes in ... God's will."
[Romans 8:26-27 / 1 Corinthians 14:2]

SPEAKING IN TONGUES IS UNDERSTOOD BY GOD
"He that speaks in an unknown tongue, speaks unto God."
[1 Corinthians 14:2]

SPEAKING IN TONGUES BUILDS YOU UP IN A SUPERNATURAL WAY
"He that speaks in an unknown tongue edifies himself."
[1 Corinthians 14:4]

SPEAKING IN TONGUES MAY BE DONE ANYTIME OUTSIDE THE CHURCH
"I speak with tongues more than all of you."
[1 Corinthians 14:18]

SPEAKING IN TONGUES SHOULD BE INTERPRETED INSIDE THE CHURCH
"And let someone interpret."
[1 Corinthians 14:27-28]

SPEAKING IN TONGUES WITH INTERPRETATION BUILDS UP THE CHURCH
" ... so that the church may receive edifying."
[1 Corinthians 14:5]

SPEAKING IN TONGUES CAN BE A SIGN TO UNBELIEVERS
"Tongues are for a sign ... to the unbeliever."
[1 Corinthians 14:22]

SPEAKING IN TONGUES IS A WAY TO SUPERNATURALLY PRAISE GOD
"They heard them speaking in tongues and praising God."
[Acts 10:44-46]

YOU CAN RECEIVE THE HOLY SPIRIT BY THE LAYING ON OF HANDS
"They laid their hands on them, and they received the Holy Spirit."
[Acts 8:17]

YOU CAN RECEIVE THE HOLY SPIRIT BY PRAYING
"Your Father in Heaven will give the Holy Spirit to them who ask."
[Luke 11:13]

Have you ever been "baptized" in the Holy Spirit? If not, ask the Lord Jesus to baptize you ... **now!** Pray and wait on God until you receive this **power!** Tell the Lord how much you love him. Praise Him! While you are praising Him, simply stop speaking your language (English) and start praising him in a new language the Holy Spirit will give you.

You will not understand your new language (neither will anyone else, unless it happens to be a language they know), but don't let that bother you. The Holy Bible says, *"The one who speaks in tongues does not speak to men ... but to God, because no one understands him. He is speaking secret truths by the power of the Spirit."* [1 Co. 14:2] Pray to God much in your new language. It will build you up, and then you will be able to build others up. 1 Corinthians 14:4 says, *"The person who speaks in tongues edifies (or, builds up) himself ..."*

✚

For in-depth research on the Holy Spirit Baptism—and the resultant gifts—study the unabridged book by Prince Handley titled, **How to Receive God's Power with Gifts of the Spirit**, available at Amazon and other book stores.

How to Prosper

THE FIRST MAN, ADAM, DISOBEYED GOD, BRINGING DEATH TO ALL MEN

"By one man, sin entered into the world, and death by sin."
[Romans 5:12]

JESUS CHRIST, THE "GOD-MAN," OBEYED GOD, BRINGING LIFE

"By the obedience of one shall many be made righteous."
[Romans 5:19]

CHRIST IS THE SON OF GOD WHO CAME TO EARTH IN HUMAN FLESH

"For God so loved the world, that he gave his only ... son."
[John 3:16]

GOD'S SON WAS BEATEN AND NAILED TO A WOODEN CROSS FOR YOU

"So Christ was once offered to bear the sins of many."
[Hebrew 9:28]

29

CHRIST DIED TO PAY FOR YOUR SINS: GOD RAISED HIM FROM THE DEAD

"Christ died for our sins ... was buried ... rose again."
[2 Corinthians 15:3-4]

IF YOU WORK WITH HIM, YOU CAN PROSPER AND BE RICH

"He became poor, that you by his poverty might be rich."
[2 Corinthians 8:9]

GOD HAS A PROGRAM: A PLAN FOR YOU TO WORK WITH HIM

"Go into all the world, and preach the Good news."
[Mark 16:15]

REMEMBER GOD AND HIS PROGRAM ON EARTH ... WORK WITH HIM

"For it is God who gives you power to get wealth."
[Deuteronomy 8:18]

WHY DOES GOD GIVE YOU POWER TO GET WEALTH?

"That he may establish his promised program."
[Deuteronomy 8:18]

GOD'S PROGRAM TAKES MONEY: FOR HIS WORKERS AND MATERIALS

"Bring all the tithes (10% of income) and prove me says the Lord."
[Malachi 3:10]

YOU CAN GIVE TO GOD BY GIVING TO
THOSE WHO PREACH THE GOSPEL
"Those who preach the Good News should live from it."
[1 Corinthians 9:14]

WHAT WILL GOD DO WHEN YOU PAY HIM TITHES
(10 % OF INCOME)?
"Pour you out a blessing ... and rebuke (Satan) the
devourer."
[Malachi 3:10-11]

YOU STEAL FROM GOD WHEN YOU DO NOT
PAY TITHES & GIVE TO HIM
"You are cursed ... you have robbed me (in tithes and
offerings)."
[Malachi 3:8-9]

HOW DOES GOD BLESS YOU
WHEN YOU OBEY HIM?
"The Lord shall open unto you his good treasure."
[Deuteronomy 28:12]

GOD WANTS YOU TO PROSPER AND
WORK WITH HIM TO HELP OTHERS
"Prosper and be in good health, just like your soul
prospers."
[3 John 2]

TRUE PROSPERITY AND SUCCESS
ONLY COME FROM KNOWING CHRIST
"What profit, if a man gains the whole world and loses
his soul?"
[Matthew 6:26]

ASK CHRIST INTO YOUR LIFE *NOW*
START LIVING AND GIVING TO GOD
"There is no other name under heaven ... whereby we
must be saved."
[Acts 4:12]

MAINTAINING PROSPERITY

TO MAINTAIN PROSPERITY, LET CHRIST & HIS PEACE RULE YOUR HOUSE
"He that troubles his own house shall inherit the wind."
[Proverb 11:29]

PUT CHRIST FIRST, EVEN IF YOU HAVE TO LEAVE FAMILY OR PROPERTY
"You will receive 100 times as much in this life, and eternal life."
[Mark 10:28-30]

DO NOT WORSHIP IDOLS—PUT GOD FIRST AND MAKE MONEY SERVE YOU
"You cannot serve both God and money."
[Luke 16:13 / Exodus 20:3]

HELP POOR PEOPLE, ORPHANS, & WIDOWS IF YOU WANT TO PROSPER
"For the Lord will plead their cause."
[Proverb 22:16, 23 / James 1:27]

DO NOT ASSOCIATE WITH PEOPLE IN WITCHCRAFT OR THE OCCULT
"All that do these things are abomination to the Lord."
[Deuteronomy 18:10-12]

LIVE FOR GOD—DO NOT TRUST IN RICHES
"He that trusts in riches shall fall ... the righteous shall flourish."
[Proverb 11:28]

BE A GOOD MANAGER: WORK HARD DEVELOP WHAT GOD GIVES YOU
"Watch your herds ... a lazy man is soon poor."
[Proverbs 10:4-5 / 27:23]

MAKE WISE DECISIONS—ASK GOD FOR WISDOM TO WORK WITH HIM
"If any of your lacks wisdom, ask God ... it will be given."
[James 1:5]

JESUS CHRIST WANTS YOU PROSPEROUS AND FREE—HE IS YOUR FRIEND
"I have come that they might have life ... abundantly."
[John 10:10]

GOD WANTS YOU TO BE A PROSPEROUS LEADER
"Be the head and not the tail ... loan ... and not borrow."
[Deuteronomy 28:12-13]

GOD DOES NOT WANT YOU TO BORROW
"The borrower is servant to the lender."
[Proverb 22:7]

YOU CAN "GIVE" YOURSELF OUT OF
ANY PROBLEM OR DEBT
"Give, and it shall be given unto you."
[Luke 6:38]

IF YOU NEED MONEY, *GIVE* MONEY
IF YOU NEED HELP, *GIVE* HELP
"Whatever a man sows, that shall he also reap."
[Galatians 6:7]

SOMETIMES GOD MAY ASK YOU TO LEAVE
YOUR JOB OR BUSINESS
"The Lord is able to give you much more than this."
[2 Chronicles 25:9]

GOD WILL LEAD YOU BY THE WAY
AND TEACH YOU HOW TO PROFIT
"I am the Lord your God which teaches you to profit."
[Isaiah 48:17]

HOW WILL GOD SUPPLY AND
MEET ALL YOUR NEEDS?
"According to his (own) riches … by Christ Jesus."
[Philippians 4:19]

GOD WILL MEET YOUR NEEDS
AND GIVE YOU GOOD THINGS
"No good thing will God hold back from them that walk
uprightly."
[Psalm 84:11]

**IF YOU DELIGHT YOURSELF IN THE LORD,
WHAT WILL GOD GIVE YOU?**
"He will give you the desires of your heart."
[Psalm 37:4]

⊥

HOW TO WIN

"To lose" means "to forfeit or to waste." "To lose" is the opposite of "to win." In the Olympic games, the goal is "to win." It is the same in the Big Game: the game of life.

To lose your life means to forfeit your life, or, to waste your life. To win life is to gain life. **You need to know HOW TO WIN—every day—forever!**

Satan, the devil (who is a very real being), came to steal from you, to kill you, and to destroy you: **the devil wants you to lose.** Jesus Christ came to earth to give you life ABUNDANTLY: **Jesus wants you to win!**

Every religious leader that has died is still dead: Confucius, Mohammed, Buddha, Krishna. None of them made it out of the grave or came back to life. Jesus Christ did! **Jesus was raised from the dead.** Jesus did not come to earth to be a religious leader. He came to give you life, so that you can win!

The first man who lived on earth was named Adam. He disobeyed God and, instead, obeyed Satan. That is how sin and death entered into the world. **God is the source of life**. When Adam, as the head of the human race, separated mankind from God, he brought death.

God loves you and sent his son Jesus Christ to earth to pay for your sins. Sin causes you to lose—to forfeit—to fail. <u>Sin separates you from God</u>. **God sent his son to heal the separation**. Jesus willingly died on the cross—beaten and nailed to it—as **the final "one-time" supreme sacrifice for the sins of the world**.

Christ died to pay for the sins of the human race. He shed his life's blood on the cross as **payment** for your sins. His blood was **holy**. He was perfect God and perfect man. Born of a virgin, through a real miracle of the Holy Spirit, **His blood did NOT contain sin from an earthly father in Adam's seed line**. Jesus came from the Father God.

Christ's blood is sufficient payment to buy you back from the hand of the devil. God is satisfied when he sees your faith in the shed blood of Christ which bought you. Now you don't have to lose. **Now you can win**: every day, forever!

Turn away from your sins that are causing you to lose. Turn to Christ and win. **Ask Christ to save you NOW**. Ask Him into your life. The Holy Bible says, *"Whoever calls upon the name of the Lord will be saved."* Pray this prayer:

"Lord Jesus, I want to win the game of life. I know you're alive and that your blood paid for my sins. Save me! Forgive my sins; I turn away from them. Lead me on earth and take me to Heaven when I die."

SUMMARY

Make sure you know **How To Win**. Nothing else will matter in this life—or eternity—unless you know **How To Win**. It is placed last in this book for two reasons:

1. To make sure you **understand WHY God sent Messiah Jesus**; and,

2. To provide you with a **resource to give to others** (by Email or regular mail or in person.)

You will want to speak the affirmations in this book often aloud (listen to yourself speaking them ... or, record them and play them back). Focus on the areas of need in your life ... or in the lives of others for which you are praying.

You may want to choose select verses from each of the sections of the book: those that speak to your heart.

✚

I have seen many MIRACLES claiming this promise from GOD:

"Call to me and I will answer you, and show you great and mighty things which you do not know."
– Tanakh: Jeremiah 33:3

OTHER BOOKS BY PRINCE HANDLEY

- Map of the End Times
- How to Do Great Works
- Flow Chart of Revelation
- Action Keys for Success
- Health and Healing Complete Guide to Wholeness
- Prophetic Calendar for Israel & the Nations: Thru 2023
- Healing Deliverance
- How to Receive God's Power with Gifts of the Spirit
- Healing for Mental and Physical Abuse
- Victory Over Opposition and Resistance
- Healing of Emotional Wounds
- How to Be Healed and Live in Divine Health
- Healing from Fear, Shame and Anger
- How to Receive Healing and Bring Healing to Others
- New Global Strategy: Enabling Missions
- The Art of Christian Warfare
- Success Cycles and Secrets
- New Testament Bible Studies (A Study Manual)
- Babylon the Bitch – Enemy of Israel
- Resurrection Multiplication – Miracle Production
- Faith and Quantum Physics – Your Future
- Conflict Healing – Relational Health
- Decision Making 101 – Know for Sure

AVAILABLE AT AMAZON AND OTHER BOOK STORES

UNIVERSITY OF EXCELLENCE PRESS
Los Angeles ◼ London ◼ Tel Aviv

BONUS

To help you, and to help you teach others, we have prepared Rabbinical Studies at this site:

www.uofe.org/RABBINICAL_STUDIES.html

These are commentaries from **ancient** Jewish Rabbis that identify the Mashiach of Israel.

To help you, and to help you teach others, we have also prepared Bible Studies in English, Spanish and French.

■ English FREE Bible Studies

www.uofe.org/english_bible_studies.html

■ Spanish FREE Bible Studies

www.uofe.org/spanish_bible_studies.html

■ French FREE Bible Studies

www.uofe.org/french_bible_studies.html

Total Person Toolbox was created for your success. Next, you will want to study in depth these three books:

How to Do Great Works

Action Keys for Success

Success Cycles and Secrets

Nothing will be able to stop YOU from MEGA success!

■ ■ ■

Email for seminars to: princehandley@gmail.com

NOTE

We listen to our readers. Tell us what **new** subject matter you would like to see published. Email your ideas to: universityofexcellence@gmail.com

UNIVERSITY OF EXCELLENCE PRESS